The Girl From Bhubaneswar

Acasa : Where you are. "One Girl, Twenty -
one Words"

Sudharsan V

BookLeaf
Publishing

India | USA | UK

Dedication

To the girl I met at Bhubaneswar Railway Station,
who unknowingly stepped into my life like the rising
sun.

To the one who walked beside me to the sacred steps of
Puri Jagannath Temple,
turning a moment into a memory, and a memory into a
meaning.

These 21 poems are not just words—they are pieces of
my heart,
a countdown of emotions, written every 30 minutes on
your birthday,
hoping that by the 21st note, you'd feel the depth of
what I feel for you.

This book is for you—
my sunshine, my fairy, my soulshine.
And one day, if destiny allows,
my forever.

Preface

This book was never planned.
It began with a moment—unexpected, magical, and deeply personal.
At Bhubaneswar Railway Station, I met her.
We shared a walk, a journey to the sacred city of Puri, and unknowingly... a story began.

These 21 poems were written across 21 days,
each one inspired by a word I used to greet her every morning.
Each word carried a piece of how I saw her—gentle, fierce, magical, real.
From Sunshine to Acasa, they form the emotional arc of a love that grew in silence,
with hope blooming in every pause.

This book is my heart's quiet confession,
a story that continues to unfold with every memory we create...
and every one we're still waiting to make.

Acknowledgements

First, I thank her—the muse, the magic, the meaning.
You gave me inspiration without even trying.
Without you, these pages would have remained empty.

To Lord Jagannath, for blessing me with a journey that
began with His name on our lips.
The spiritual air of Puri still lingers in my words.

To the railway station that became a crossroad,
where a Tamil boy met his Odia girl and everything
quietly changed.

To my own heart—for feeling deeply, writing honestly,
and daring to hope.

And finally, to every reader holding this book—
May you find your own reflection in these verses,
and may love, in its most delicate and powerful form,
find its way to you too.

Day 1. Sunshine

I saw you first beneath a sky so wide,
The station bustled, but you paused beside.
A gentle smile, my heartbeat's spark,
You lit my grey world with a golden mark.

Sunshine, you stood—radiant, divine,
In that fleeting moment, the stars aligned.
You didn't know then what you became—
The warmth behind my every name.

Day 2. Buttercup

You laughed like spring, in a yellow breeze,
Soft like petals, swaying with ease.
You hummed a tune near Jagannath's gate,
Buttercup bright, you rewrote my fate.

I watched you giggle, eyes so free,
As if the gods had sent you to me.
A memory pressed like a flower's cup—
Delicate, sweet, my Buttercup.

Day 3. Fairy

Not all wings flutter, not all spells shine,
But you, my Fairy, cast a line.
A glance, a word, a silent smile—
You turned my doubts to dreams worthwhile.

You walked beside me, just a few steps—
But each one etched like sacred texts.
Invisible dust from your passing feet—
A fairy's presence, pure and sweet.

Day 4. Snowflake

You melted softly into my life,
Unique in pattern, without strife.
A brief encounter, cold yet kind,
Like a snowflake you touched my mind.

No two the same, they say of snow—
And yet, in you, the rarest glow.
You didn't stay, but still you stick—
A frozen wish, a gentle flick.

Day 5. Rosebud

You weren't the rose that screamed with bloom,
But a rosebud held in morning gloom.
Quiet, unsure, not yet shown—
But in that silence, fully grown.

You stood in prayer, eyes so deep—
The temple watched, the gods did keep.
A rose yet wrapped in layers spun—
But still, for me, the only one.

Day 6. Marshmallow

Soft were your words, like evening's hush,
Your kindness came in a sudden rush.
Like marshmallows melting in warm delight,
You softened the edges of my night.

You didn't know the weight I bore,
But you smiled, and I asked for more.
No bitterness, no rush, no show—
Just you, and your silent marshmallow glow.

Day 7. Pretty

They say beauty lies in how we see—
And pretty was how you looked at me.
Not makeup, not clothes, not hair tied tight,
But pretty in soul, quiet and light.

You helped a child, you folded a hand,
Your kindness bloomed where few would stand.
And I stood still, completely smitten—
By the prettiest verse I'd never written.

Day 8. Firefly

You blinked into my life, so small,
A firefly's glow that outshone all.
You lit the dark, not with pride—
But with the truth you couldn't hide.

In temple lamps and coastal breeze,
I found you in the simplest peace.
You didn't linger, but I still try—
To chase that light, my firefly.

Day 9. Twinkle

Twinkle in your teasing eye,
When you turned and waved goodbye.
I laughed alone, my heart half-won—
Like spotting stars in morning sun.

Twinkle in the things unsaid,
In the wishes spinning through my head.
Did you know you left a trace?
A universe behind your face.

Day 10. Aurora

A northern light in an eastern dawn,
You rose where myths and prayers are drawn.
Aurora soul, rare and bright,
You painted silence with dancing light.

I stood in shadows, unsure and still,
But you burst forth with gentle will.
I knew then what I hoped before—
You were something I'd adore.

Day 11. Lifeline

That day, I missed my train of thought,
You lingered—everything I forgot.
My lifeline looped into your thread,
You spoke in ways no word had said.

A friend, a muse, a quiet song—
You helped me feel where I felt wrong.
Though distance came, your mark remains—
Like rivers locked in lover's veins.

Day 12. Soul Shine

Not skin-deep love, not surface glare,
But soul shine glowing everywhere.
You didn't boast, you didn't try—
But still, you caught my inward eye.

You knew the temple, knew the tides,
But deeper still, you knew the sides
Of people broken, yet alive—
You shone where others just survive.

Day 13. Jaan / Heartbeat

You became my Jaan, my beat unknown,
In silence, your presence alone had grown.
We didn't hold, we didn't kiss—
But still, you filled what life would miss.

Heartbeat fast in temple smoke,
In every smile, in every joke.
Even now, in dreams you start—
And walk again inside my heart.

Day 14. Lucky Charm / Dream girl

You are my dream girl, soft and rare,
My lucky charm with temple prayer.
The world might call this fleeting fate,
But I hold on, and hope, and wait.

You carried grace in steps so small,
And yet, you made me feel so tall.
For every wish I've ever made—
You're the girl I never trade.

Day 15. Pookie / Honeybee

Yes, I saved your name that day—
As "Pookie", in a playful way.
A nickname born without a plan,
Yet sweeter than the sweetest jam.

Like honeybee drawn to a bloom,
You danced around, erased my gloom.
You buzzed a song into my chest—
Of silly names and silent rest.

Day 16. Ikigai

You gave me reason, gave me why,
Like breath beneath a clearer sky.
You didn't ask, you didn't know—
But still, you made my purpose grow.

Ikigai, my morning spark,
You brought the light into my dark.
Not forever, not for show—
But enough to make my spirit glow.

Day 17. Samvaer

In quiet, you were near to me—
Samvaer, our silent symphony.
We didn't talk the longest hours,
But shared the air, the temple flowers.

Together yet untouched by time,
A closeness built without a rhyme.
We sat, we breathed, we both just knew—
There's something sacred in me and you.

Day 18. Mi Cielo

Mi Cielo—my sky, so high,
Your gaze like clouds that learn to fly.
Above my world, you gently float,
On whispered dreams I never wrote.

You were not mine, and still you stayed—
As constellations never fade.
My heaven sent, my language lost—
But worth the wait, whatever the cost.

Day 19. Mo Chroi

Mo Chroi—you're my heart in Irish hue,
A phrase for love that feels so true.
We didn't touch, we didn't swear,
But still, my soul felt you were there.

In crowded trains and darshan lines,
I lost my place but found the signs.
My heart was yours, though unaware—
Mo Chroi, my sacred prayer.

Day 20. Mysa

You brought me peace I never knew,
A soft retreat from what I do.
In your voice, I found my rest—
In Mysa moments, I felt blessed.

No grand escape, no loud goodbyes,
Just temple winds and starlit skies.
You were my pause, my sacred space—
My Mysa warmth, my slowing pace.

Day 21. Acasa

I'm still searching trains and skies,
Still whispering to the gods and highs.
For one more chance, one gentle trace—
Of you, my home, my Acasa place.

I'll meet you again, in steps we missed,
In temple bells or twilight mist.
You are not gone, just far today—
But in my heart, you always stay.

Final. A Day My Heart Keeps Replaying

A Day My Heart Keeps Replaying

I could write you a poem, pages filled with metaphors
and rhymes...
But sometimes, just remembering a moment is poetry
enough.
I may not be a permanent name in your story,
But let me be a beautiful chapter — short, but
unforgettable.

That day, I saw you again after a long time...
At Master Canteen bus stop, you were looking for me,
texting, searching.
But I had already seen you — walking with grace,
unaware of the chaos you stirred in my heart.
Your friend looked startled when I approached,
But then you smiled... and she did too.
That one smile — like the universe paused for a second
just for me.

The train journey to Puri was something I'll never forget.
You sat beside me, and somewhere between stations and
small talks,
You offered me biscuits.
Simple? Maybe.
But to me, it felt like sharing a part of your world.

When we got off the train and waited for your friend,
I gave you a tissue to wipe the dust off your face.
You worried about your kajal fading.
I said, "Next time, I'll bring you eyeliner."
You laughed — and that laughter still echoes somewhere
inside me.

When boys got too close to your friend,
You instinctively pulled her closer.
And I, from the other side, stepped in quietly to shield
you both.
You didn't ask... but I was there.
You were protective. I was present.

We'd finished the biscuits, and hunger was catching up
with your friend.
We searched for food, found none.
So we entered the Jagannath Temple — my very first
time.

And what a feeling...
They say you feel something divine there. I did.
Not just because of the God inside,
But maybe because you were beside me.

The crowd grew tighter. Your friend went ahead.
I noticed you weren't able to see the deity clearly.
So I blocked the crowd, gently guided us closer to the
pole,
Letting you have your moment — uninterrupted.
And when you finally looked at me — no words, just
your eyes —
That one silent glance said more than an entire
conversation ever could.

I was coughing, breathless in that narrow path,
But I didn't mind. I had seen you smile in a place filled
with divinity.
We had Maha Prasad —
You shared a plate with your friend, and I watched with
quiet envy.
You even let me eat from the same plate...
A stranger, from another state.
That gesture... more intimate than most people would
understand.

You refused to drink water while eating —

Something about your belief, your practice.
I respected it.
And somewhere deep down, wished to be part of even
those small habits of yours.

We tied wishes to the tree,
I balanced a coin on the wall and whispered mine.
I bought a flag, the same color flying high above the
temple —
A piece of that day, a symbol I still hold onto.

On the way back, I accidentally stepped on your skirt.
I apologized immediately, feeling awful.
But you just smiled. Like it didn't matter.
That kindness... it disarmed me completely.

We took pictures together —
In front of Jagannath, the universal God.
I didn't know if I'd get a photo with you that day,
But somehow, without a word, it just happened.
You stood beside me.
She clicked the picture.
No planning, no posing — just a moment that fell
perfectly into place.

I wanted to take one of you both too...
But time slipped past us quietly, and we walked on.

The plan for Puri beach was left behind,
Time didn't wait.
Neither did my flight.
As I sat in the auto, mind spinning and heart heavy,
I said, "See you..."
But inside, I didn't want to go.
Not yet.

I reached just in time for my flight.
Maybe because of your prayers. Maybe God's grace.
But that day — every frame, every smile, every pause —
It still plays in my head, more than a hundred times.

And now, on your birthday, I have just one wish:
Let's make another memory.
A temple, a beach, another train ride — just us.
No rush, no flight to catch.
Just one more day like that.

Am I allowed to take you?
No — not take...
Am I allowed to kidnap you for a temple and beach day?
You just fix the date. I'll take care of the rest.